tranquil thoughts

on pregnancy

Kattrin Davida

tranquil thoughts

on pregnancy

introduction

What will it be? A boy? A girl?
What seed is this that has been
planted? A mustard perhaps?
Or a poppy? It's hard to tell.
Only when it flowers will we know.

Pregnancy is one of the great mysteries of
life and there is no one who goes into it
without feeling a little apprehensive, and
probably more than a little concerned
about how it is likely to turn out. It can fill
our heads with all manner of questions
and we cannot stop analyzing why we
wanted to do it in the first place. We

wonder whether or not we will make good mothers, and, most fundamentally of all, whether we will be up to the challenges. For every bad tale about pregnancy there are thousands of good tales, and as for endings? Well, pregnancy has got more to do with happy beginnings. It's the beginning of a whole new life, not only for the child we carry inside us, but for us too. When we become pregnant we start a whole new phase in our lives that would otherwise pass us by. We begin to see the world and everything in it as though for the very first time, and we view anything as possible. Our life on this planet may have started some time ago, but the moment we discover we are pregnant is the moment that we really begin to live it.

eation miracle

Pregnancy is probably the most wonderful miracle we here on earth can experience, for those of us who are pregnant and everyone we come into contact with. We are all part of the miracle of creation. A baby is conceived through an act of love— whether it is helped along the way by science or not. Love generates new life and all the ordeals of pregnancy are turned into joy and ecstasy.

"Do not forget to entertain strangers, for by so doing some have unwittingly entertained angels unawares."

The Bible

Now your body, the pride and joy of your being, your shop front to the world, is no longer exclusively yours. For the next nine months it is to be shared with another— a complete stranger, someone you have never seen before, whom you have never known—and yet it feels absolutely right and normal. Within the tiny space that you have struggled to maintain at a certain size and shape through diets and exercise, another human being is about to grow. A full-sized baby will pop out into the bigger world that you inhabit and share the rest of your life with you as the closest being you will ever know.

a visitor

free
time

It doesn't all have to go like clockwork. There's no need
to know exactly when the baby is due—it will let you
know when the time is right. But you do have to make a
choice about whether you are going to let your pregnancy
tie you down, or whether you see it as the most freeing
event a woman can possibly experience. You are free to
use your body as nature intended, to do the most
wonderful thing a human being can do. In this complex
world some choose to protest for peace, but right now
you are a walking endorsement for love and life.

Ask any woman about the moment when she discovered she was pregnant and she will recall it in an instant. However we discover we are pregnant it always comes as a bombshell. Whether

astonishing

it's the thin blue line on a drugstore predictor kit, a formal postal result from a laboratory, or your doctor telling you in person, it always happens suddenly. Whether you were expecting it or not, there it is—confirmed. The results are positive. You are pregnant! Congratulations! Suddenly a thousand questions spring into your head and behind them a thousand more join the queue. You stand there dazed while every emotion in the book seems to flood into your body as if loading themselves into position for future attacks. What on earth happens now? The first thing to do is to relax and, using a mirror, look yourself in the eye and say these words: "I am going to have a baby!"

news

now what?

The need to know what to do next can be all-consuming. We want to do it right. What should we read? What should we buy? The anxiety level rises and, as we grasp at straws looking for clues, we must learn to relax. We must remember that there have been countless mothers before us and there will be countless more mothers and babies to follow. For now, what we have to do most of all is shut out all those pressures and influences and get to grips with ourselves. After all, we have a baby who will want to know who we are and it would be useful, perhaps, if we knew too.

taking control

Some women feel as though they are trapped in a sequence of events over which they have no control, and to some extent this is true. But if you think about it, you do have choices all the way along the line—your choices. From choosing whether or not to get pregnant in the first place, to how you look, feel, and deal with it, up until how it is born and the level of comfort you are prepared to accept—these are free will choices that we all have. It's about taking the lead role in your pregnancy, and not being led down the path of overbearing specialists and old wives' tales.

"What man's mind can create, man's character can control."

Thomas A. Edison

touchstones

Your body is never going to look and feel this way again. Collect some souvenirs of the journey.

Try to get some video footage or at least some photographs of yourself in all your pregnant glory. Some women even go so far as to have a plaster cast made of their bellies, which they can display proudly. For a mom who loves to talk about her pregnancy experiences, it's a wonderful way to get the conversation going. Otherwise, your souvenirs can simply be a talisman in quiet times, to help you reflect upon that incredible journey you took with your child to get to where you are today.

telling others

One of the greatest sources of fun throughout pregnancy will be finding ways of breaking the news to others, while taking a few safety precautions at the same time. Cars have been known to run off roads and people have nearly drowned in the bath on receiving the news. As exciting as it may seem to hire a sky-writing plane to display it in the clouds while you and your partner sunbathe on a beach below, the moment should feel right to you, and when it does present itself, just do it. Where there is love, there will always be an excellent response—even if it is momentarily delayed by angst, panic, choking, tears, or whatever else.

The smile should follow, and the warm embrace.

Those who care for you will just want you to be happy.

We have indisputable evidence of the incredible psychological and hormonal changes that are taking place within us, but spare a thought for our partners— the expectant dads who have nothing to show for all the new thoughts and feelings they're going through. Does

unseen pregnancy

he feel ready to become a father? What if it's a girl?

Or a boy? Or both! Our bump grows, friends even talk to it and ask us questions, but poor fathers spend this momentous period worrying about money, the future, and the state of the home, as well as our well-being, and the baby. Make sure you talk to each other about both of your feelings and anxieties. It will draw you even closer.

You're pregnant. You have been granted a license to thrill! Whether it is tight stretch satin or a frilly nursery style you go for, the world will accept it because you are having a baby. Now is the time to make a statement, to be outrageous, or simply to have a bit of fun. Your body is about to undergo a major change—a number of major changes—and it would be a great shame to pretend it isn't happening and to try to hide it all.

licensed to thrill

Celebrate maternity with style and you'll be amazed at the variety that's out there waiting for an adventuress like you.

food for thought

Pregnancy cravings are perfectly natural. Sudden middle-of-the-night urges come over us and strange food combinations suggest themselves to us. Without understanding why, we can find ourselves dashing out for dill pickles and sour cream, roast chicken and chocolate sauce. While we shouldn't necessarily give in to all of them, we should pay attention to our pregnancy cravings, and our aversions too. They're usually more interesting than problematic. Indulge a few. But, most importantly, make sure that you have lots of emotional support around you because the tides of emotions that accompany pregnancy can cause us to turn to food when all we really need is a great big hug.

Choosing a name for a baby is a strange pastime. Consider for a moment that during one of the most irrational times of our own lives, we are going to try to create the handle our offspring will carry with them throughout their entire lives. There is a lot of fashion involved in names and while it might be stylish to be a Caroline spelled "Karolygn" for effect, or while Bartholomew might sound sophisticated in its long form, these children will grow to see their names either misspelled or mispronounced for years to come or will have them shortened to fractions of the original like Bart.

baby names

unfamiliar territory

Motherhood is a whole new world filled with exciting gadgets and gizmos, shapes, and colors, and it's never too early to walk into the baby department and explore just what's on offer. These are the sights and sounds, the equipment, your kit—your tools of the trade. Get used to them; familiarize yourself with the territory that comes with parenting. It's never too early to

learn how to unfold a buggy,
to put up a mobile, or to
practise reading aloud.

Let your mind fill with thoughts of love—the love of others for you, and your love for your growing child. Let your heart and mind free themselves from all the preoccupations of daily life.

we two

No matter how strange the feeling is now, with all these great changes, at this pregnant moment, allow your thoughts to turn and your heart to guide you to your child. You are never alone—there is now, and always will be, the two of you.

drifting along

Some women seem to choose, not to enjoy their pregnancy, but to torment themselves with stories of others' past pregnancies and to fill themselves with apprehensions of all the awful things that may happen. If we all felt like this, no children would be born at all. Finding happiness while carrying such anxieties is like trying to make a rock float. Instead, think positively, and learn to relax. Create a calm atmosphere for yourself and your baby. Imagine you are a feather floating on the surface of still water.

Each day pregnant is like a separate life in its own right.

faith, doubt, and effort

If you do not get your courage from yourself, where, then, will you go for it? It takes great courage to get beyond all the doubt and to decide to become pregnant. Rest assured that where there is great doubt, there will be a great awakening; where there is small doubt, a small awakening; and where there is no doubt at all, there can be no awakening.

do the right thing

There is a place for well-meaning advice, but we also have to discover for ourselves.

Every mother is keen to impart to her daughter the lessons that she has learnt about pregnancy and motherhood. But they must also understand that they should refrain from meddling while we try to make sense of the experience for ourselves—we

need to go our own way with it. Of course it's good to know that they are there for us and we do have room in our pregnancy for kind and helpful words, but we do have to do this for ourselves and try to understand the reasons why we make each of our choices.

waking tiger

When we are pregnant we begin to experience intense
feelings and fears that weren't familiar to us before.
Once awakened, they are impossible to ignore and we
must learn to accept them as a normal part of
pregnancy. Each of us will find our own way of coming
to terms with what we experience. With a basic
understanding of the physical and emotional changes
we are likely to encounter, and with
the support of our family, partners,
and friends, our pregnancy should be
a positive experience. There are many
things common to all pregnancies,
but for each
woman,
her own
pregnancy
is unique.

a tale of great daring

When a woman gets pregnant, she must be ready to risk her body, to risk her well-being, to risk her life, in the great event of childbirth. We deserve all the credit we can get for bearing children, because we are the ones in the arena facing the lions. Our blood is shed, our tears fall, as we strive valiantly to give birth to each new generation. We may make mistakes en route but who knows better than us of the great devotion involved? After all, we spend ourselves for this worthy cause so we should be triumphant about our achievement.

If you want to see paradise, then
go and take a good long look at
your naked pregnant body in the
mirror. There you will realize
three things: that there can be
no paradise where there is not
life; that life IS paradise; and
that at this moment in time
you are in fact two lives. It may
not feel that way in the early

paradise found

months of pregnancy, but when
you feel your baby move, you
will realize that what you began is now its own self.

listen well

Books are helpful and joining groups or classes widens our social circle and can provide us with confidence, but don't forget to allow yourself space to dwell on the wonderful side of pregnancy—the magic of it all. Bathe in the incredible oneness of being a mother together with her infant growing inside her. If a pregnant woman wants to be on the receiving end of information then the very best source is to listen to your child, who, if you are listening carefully, will communicate with you via little body messages, pulses, temperature changes, and even moods—a kick from within, perhaps.

metamorphoses

Some of us enter pregnancy thinking like a caterpillar. We see ourselves as some kind of protective cocoon out of which will come a butterfly and, at that stage, our life as we knew it will be ended. In actual fact, what really happens is that two beautiful butterflies emerge after nine months— a child and a mother.

keeping

Pregnancy
requires
perseverance,
personal sacrifice,
and self-denial.

It's time to cut back on all the things we know can
harm our unborn child. Such respect provides an

it pure

instant feeling of oneness, of
dependence upon each another,
and in this rarefied atmosphere
mother and baby can derive the

strength they need from their unity to get through it
together. Being pregnant is a special kind of teamwork.

It's completely
natural for
you to feel
a confusing
array of conflicting emotions when you're pregnant. Think
about it. Your body is undergoing drastic alteration and
constantly searching for its equilibrium in this whirlwind of
change. Combine this

calm dowr

with extreme tiredness
and you might find
yourself tearful, and overwhelmed by an all-embracing feeling
of defeat. When this happens, it's time to step back, take a
deep breath, run a gentle warm bath with a few drops of
your favorite essential oil, lie back in the water, clear your
mind, and
relax.

Pregnancy is the bridge between the natural and the supernatural, between the temporal and the eternal, the now and the hereafter, the future generations and the generations that came before us.

shaking hands

with the past

Each child that is born is another link in a chain that stretches back as far as the Garden of Eden. My baby is my gift to the continuity of the species. He or she may make great contributions to society or, like me, they may raise a family and quietly contribute to the ongoing flow.

the empty vessel

Lie on a soft floor and imagine this.
We are all shaped like clay into a pot,
an empty vessel. Now consider your
pregnancy: it is the emptiness inside
that holds what you want. Be with
each other.
Picture your **Lie there breathing**
baby and **gently for a while and**
tell yourself **listen to each other.**
this: "My
heartbeat echoes around you, my
anxieties race around you like a
turbulent sea." And now find a calm
state that you can easily get back to
at any time during your pregnancy,
whenever you and your baby need it.

questions

Each moment of every day is filled with questions. What will it be—a girl or a boy, or both? Who will it look like? Will it be outgoing or shy? And what about me? Will I be a good mother? Will I know what to do? Will I be confident or timid? Then it sinks in that soon it will no longer be just me, it will be me and someone that will be totally dependent upon me. How will I feel about that? These questions are asked by every mother-to-be. Don't be overwhelmed by all that. You are your child's physical home right now—nurturing it every step of the way. Your well-being is your child's well-being.

You need to remember this:

Your happiness is your baby's happiness.

forgiveness

We are, as women, free to deliberate, to make decisions, and to choose between alternatives. Pregnancy demands a tough mind and a tender heart. In order to even consider entering into a full-term pregnancy, we must first ask ourselves whether we are prepared to develop and maintain the capacity within us to forgive. Forgive the pain, forgive the discomfort; it isn't intentional—it is all part of the process. If we can nurture the power to forgive, we are certain to have the power to love. And that is the foundation of pregnancy. Love.

strange new land

From the moment we first conceive until the moment we give birth, we become tourists in the strange and foreign land of pregnancy, where there's much to see and do and learn. It becomes clear that we are not alone, that there are others on the tour besides us with whom we can talk and share our experiences. We can and should savor every moment of it, each new discovery made along the way, and relish all the unfamiliar sensations and emotions that are part of the journey. **Collect some mementos as you go: make a few new friends and meet a few new mothers.**

Take time during your pregnancy to look around you. Observe carefully what the world you are bringing your precious baby

contemplating

into has to offer. Savor the colors, the smells, the sounds, the textures, and the shapes as though for the very first time— try to imagine them as your baby will see them. How will you explain to your little one the golden orb in the night sky or the hum of the cicada or the perfume of a rose?

the world

grandmothers

Everybody's role is about to change. Our
mothers, whether still with us or not, are
about to be grandmothers, and their mothers
will become our child's great-grandmothers—
and so the domino effect continues throughout
our family line, right back to our very earliest
ancestors. Everybody has a new part to play in the
family tree. If our mothers are physically still with
us, we will be able to watch them rejuvenate for
a while as their own memories and experiences
come flooding back. It's a very close time for all
mothers and daughters as they await the arrival
of the new member of the family.

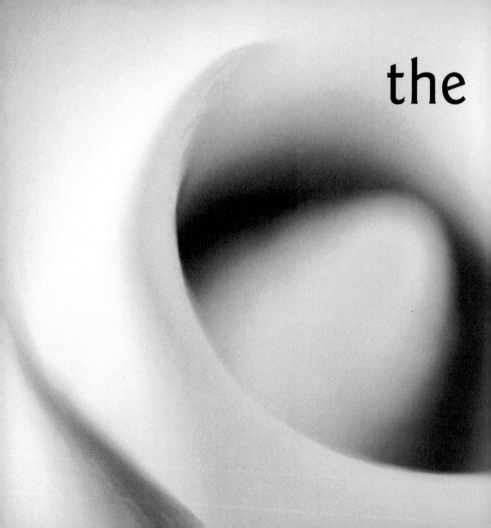

the

meeting

It's more nerve-wracking than a first date—a blind date at that! For nine months we have been communicating regularly with someone whom we have never even seen. Yet we have grown very fond, if not deeply in love with them. Now we are rapidly approaching the extraordinary moment that will bring the two of us together for the very first time. So focus on that and think about who it is you are about to meet.

When you finally come face to face, sing "Happy Birthday" to your baby, because that's just what it is. A birth day.

Our body seems to have taken on a life of its own. The question rises within us: "Can I retain my looks and, more importantly, will I ever be able to get back to the way I was before?" The terrifying thought creeps in that our body, which we have given over to house this other little human—with birthing and nursing still to come—may never belong to us again. We think that we'll somehow  be trapped inside the crinkled wrapping paper of someone else's gift. Nonsense. With a bit of exercise and effort we'll soon be back on form.

shaping a life

fear of the birth

"Heaven grant that the burden you carry may have as easy an exit as it had an entrance."

Desiderius Erasmus

At some point we begin to ask the question: "Am I prepared for all this?" Much focus is placed upon the pains of birth, but speak with any mothers and they will tell you it is all worthwhile. In any case, the experience has receded so far back in their memory that they cannot recall anything but greeting their baby. Perhaps we too can put these thoughts to the back of our minds and focus upon learning how to relax... relax... relax.

quickening

Things have quietened down a little now. The morning sickness may have eased, and the worry about not getting through has decreased. This is the time when we will suddenly be caught by the surprise of feeling Junior moving about within us. Once that fetus flips everything begins to feel so very real—it all becomes exciting and beautiful, and this in turn leads to us having increased energy and vitality. We begin to glow and dig out the maternity wear to dress for the part.

Why not take the time to rejoice in the extraordinariness of nature, that we have evolved in this orchard to be able to reproduce?

count your blessings

Is there a limit to our capabilities? It's possible to count the seeds that lie sleeping in an apple, but who can count the number of apples that lie sleeping in a seed?

anticipation

As you wait, anticipating the arrival of your infant, get
to know your pregnancy. In the scheme of things it
won't be with you long and, once gone, it can never
be revisited. What is the feel of pregnancy? The feeling
to you, of you, and of things around you? The changes
to your body and your emotions? Focus upon these.
Now consider the taste: what has changed, what do
you crave, and what do you experience? Take time to
consider the look and the sound of pregnancy, from
within and from without.

These months are all too brie

and we will never have this exact experience again.

Learn to live for each moment—not the time that has gone or the time that has not yet come. This instant is all the time there is. You can't hurry pregnancy and neither can you turn back the clock. To grow from a sapling to a young tree takes time and every moment along the way is vital in its development. This is one of the important lessons you must learn. It takes a long time to become young!

this moment in time

the

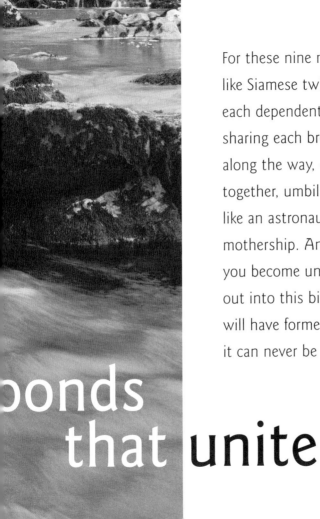

For these nine months we are like Siamese twins, you and I, each dependent upon the other, sharing each breath, each step along the way, everything we do together, umbilically joined, you like an astronaut and me the mothership. And by the time you become unattached and step out into this big world, a bond will have formed so strong that it can never be broken.

bonds
that unite

In the final weeks, anxiety mixed with discomfort can make for a potentially stressful time. Sleep is disrupted and we may feel vulnerable and undesirable. Now we need a hug, a cuddle, a kiss from our partner. Such signals of reassurance are uplifting. We need to escape the feelings of confinement, and all the fears associated with delivery, and we need to focus on the love that brought all this into being. Now is the time that our relationship with our partner can become warmer and more sensual than it has ever been. We are becoming a family, the three of us in each other's arms— safe, secure, wanted, and loved.

nearly there

week 27 to touchdown

Inside mom there is a fully kitted-out chubby baby. Mother's pride is now tinged with anxieties about what is yet to come. Seats are offered on buses, shopping bags are carried to cars, everyone becomes a bit more attentive towards her needs, and possibly she needs the help. We're not "helpless" but neither should we be offended by people's actions. They are only celebrating our pregnancy or giving some small thanks or sign of appreciation for their own birth—remembering their own mothers. They are gestures that are offered only to the privileged few. US.

the journey

Picture the long-distance runner who wants to be champion and imagine the pain barrier they must overcome in order to achieve that goal. Continue now to imagine an expedition that sets out on foot to reach the South Pole, or to climb the Himalayas, or a cyclist in the Tour de France—all have a clear goal in sight and their own pain barriers to break through to achieve them. With a good clear goal in our sights any pain or discomfort along the way becomes almost a companion—a reminder of the wonderful glittering prizes that await us at the finishing line. That's where your baby is.

nurturing

Am I prepared for pregnancy? Consider the farmer tending his land. Does he just scatter his precious seed over the ground and hope for the best? No. He chooses the best site, nurtures the soil, prepares it lovingly with fertilizers, and tills it until it is in a perfect condition to accept the seed. From that time

forth he caresses it and feeds it regularly, he roots out weeds, protects it from frosts, and keeps it watered. He keeps watch over it as the shoots poke through the ground and the plants grow tall. As a result of such loving preparation and care he can look forward to harvesting his crop—the fruits of his labor.

"Journeys end in lovers meeting."
William Shakespeare

sailing into the

One cannot get just a little bit pregnant—pregnancy is an entire voyage. It's like being at sea, sometimes enjoying fair weather and, at other times, being buffeted by the storm. Once you're aboard, there's nothing you can do except go with the flow and ride the waves. We will ask ourselves time and time again whether it was wise to cast off and set sail into unfamiliar waters. But when we reach the safety of the harbor and unload our precious cargo, we will feel blessed on the one hand and strange on the other now that the voyage has come to an end.

unknown

building
your
nest

Throughout nature, pregnancy is a time of preparation—of building dens and constructing nests—and creating comfortable havens ready to accept the arrival of new offspring. This is the ideal time to consider what will be needed to make a nurturing and peaceful environment for your baby, and to apply your skills, or recruit the skills of others, to implement your ideas. The process will be therapeutic for you and the finished result will bring the tranquillity of knowing that everything is perfectly ready.

"In a broken nest there are few whole eggs."

Chinese proverb

special madness

Being pregnant is a license to be mad and to do mad things such as talking to yourself. But then you aren't talking to yourself, are you? It is your baby that the outside world catches you having conversations with, and this is to be encouraged. Talking to your baby is just like the loving gardener talking and tending to her plants. It makes them happier and calmer. Your voice can provide comfort and stimulus, and your baby can hear you. Just try singing a soothing lullaby while you are relaxing, and from the garden inside someone may join in.

blinded
by love

Is there such a phenomenon as love at first
sight? Perhaps it's not such an
absurd notion. After all, there is
certainly love at no sight at all.
During pregnancy we form a
picture in our minds of the sort of
person our child is likely to be–
serious or happy-go-lucky, dark-
haired or fair. And in an uncanny
way, when that never-before-seen
head pops into the world we
instinctively know who it is. We
offer this total newcomer the
unrestricted, unconditional love
that no one else in our lives will ever know from us.

99

Being pregnant is the most beautiful experience in the world. It is heaven on earth, the tangible miracle of two lives growing— ours from the old "I" to the new "I", plus another "I" inside.

expecting miracles

The new "I" grows in tandem with a new life—the next generation, the child "I" gave life to. Suddenly we feel an affinity with the mighty oak standing proud and firm beside the acorn here in life's glorious field. This is a woman's finest hour, her unparalleled moment of fulfillment. We are the past, the present, and the future, all at once.

waves

As the birth approaches, it
can feel as though we are
caught in a huge tidal wave of
strange processes over which we
have no control, and many women
have anxious dreams about things
going wrong. Try to think of how a
surfer rides the waves, using their
immense power to carry him safely to
the shore. Nature is on our side and will
help us to reach our wonderful destination.
You may even find that you enjoy the ride!

pyrotechnics

Celebrate being pregnant and what is to come—who you were and who you will become. Wear your pregnant belly with pride and joy. Just as the cherry tree celebrates the birth of spring by producing swelling buds which will bloom, and bathe our life in sweet perfume, and flood our eyes with vibrant displays of frothy blossoms, so too do we signal a coming, the arrival of new life, a change in seasons— a glimpse of heaven on earth. **Pregnancy is a brilliant display.**

seeds

Some, of course, think
pregnancy far too risky an
undertaking; too big a tree to
climb, with uncertain weather
conditions, and a long way to
fall. But for others, when they
can see the fruit that is offered
way out there upon each limb,
they are prepared to go out on
it with great daring, and to
harvest the crop.

It is a brave

decision to plant the seeds of the future.

travel
through
life

Now the space within is once more ours and now there are the two of us side by side in the world of mortals, how shall our time together be best spent? What will we learn from each other as we travel through life together? Perhaps life teaches us that we should always focus upon the journey and less so upon the destination—and enjoy going together, mother and child, to where we have never gone before, each generation carrying the memories of places we have been.

Published by MQ Publications Limited
12 The Ivories
6–8 Northampton Street
London N1 2HY
Tel: +44 (0)20 7359 2244 / Fax: +44 (0)20 7359 1616
e-mail: mail@mqpublications.com
website: www.mqpublications.com

Text © 2003 Kattrin Davida
Cover image: Grace Carlon, Flowers & Foliage
Interior images: © Digital Vision

ISBN: 1-84072-468-4

10 9 8 7 6 5 4 3 2 1

Printed in China

Note on the CD

The music that accompanies this book has been specially commissioned from composer David Baird. Trained in music and drama in Wales, and on the staff of the Welsh National Opera & Drama company, David has composed many soundtracks for both the theater and radio.

The CD can be played quietly through headphones while relaxing or meditating on the text. Alternatively, lie on the floor between two speakers placed at equal distances from you. Try and center your thoughts, and allow the soundtrack to wash over you and strip away the distracting layers of the outside world.